Woodwind

Wendy Lynch

Heinemann

Schools Library and Information Services

www.heinemann.co.uk/library

Visit our website to find out more information about **Heinemann Library** books.

To order:

 Phone ++44 (0)1865 888066

 Send a fax to ++44 (0)1865 314091

 Visit the Heinemann Bookshop at www.heinemann.co.uk/library to browse our catalogue and order online.

First published in Great Britain by Heinemann Library, Halley Court, Jordan Hill, Oxford OX2 8EJ, a division of Reed Educational and Professional Publishing Ltd. Heinemann is a registered trademark of Reed Educational & Professional Publishing Ltd.

OXFORD MELBOURNE AUCKLAND JOHANNESBURG BLANTYRE
GABORONE IBADAN PORTSMOUTH NH (USA) CHICAGO

Designed by Visual Image
Originated by Dot Gradations
Printed in China

ISBN 0 431 12901 0 (hardback)   ISBN 0 431 12907 X (paperback)

06 05 04 03 02   06 05 04 03 02
10 9 8 7 6 5 4 3 2   10 9 8 7 6 5 4 3 2 1

British Library Cataloguing in Publication Data

Lynch, Wendy
    Woodwind. – (Musical instruments)
    1. Woodwind instruments – Juvenile literature
    I. Title
    788.2

Acknowledgements

The publishers would like to thank the following for permission to reproduce photographs: All Action p26, Bubbles pp13, 16 (Franz-Rombout), Collections (Michael St Maur Sheil) p20, Corbis p23, Gareth Boden pp10, 14 (and JHS & Co), 24, 28, 29, JHS & Co p15, Lebrecht collection (Chris Stock) p19, Photodisc (Cumulus) pp6, 7, Photofusion p11, 12 (Ray Roberts), Pictor pp4, 5, Pictures (Clive Sawyer) p9, Redferns (Odile Noel) p17, Rex pp18, 25, Robert Harding p21, Sally Greenhill p8, Stone p27, Travel Ink (Marc Dublin) p22.

Cover photograph reproduced with permission of Photodisc.

Every effort has been made to contact copyright holders of any material reproduced in this book. Any omissions will be rectified in subsequent printings if notice is given to the Publisher.

Any words appearing in the text in bold, **like this**, are explained in the Glossary.

Contents

Making music together

There are many musical instruments in the world. Each instrument makes a different sound. We can make music together by playing these instruments in a band or an **orchestra**.

Bands and orchestras are made up of different groups of instruments. One of these groups is called woodwind. You can see many woodwind instruments in this orchestra.

What are woodwind instruments?

These are called woodwind instruments because you blow air into them to make a sound. As you blow, a line of air pushes against the edge of the **mouthpiece** or **reed**.

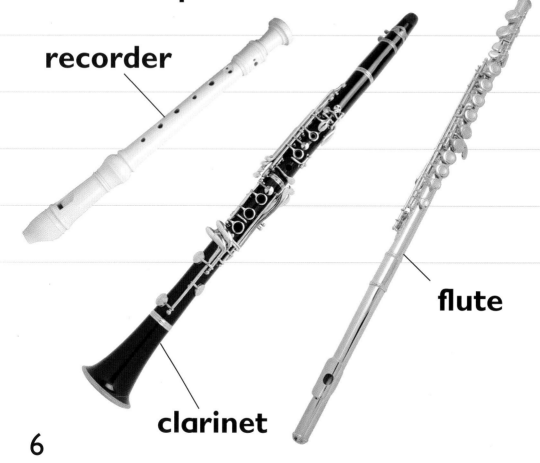

recorder

clarinet

flute

They are also called woodwind instruments because they all used to be made of wood. Now the flute and the saxophone are made of silver or brass.

bassoon

saxophone

oboe

The recorder

The recorder is a woodwind instrument. The recorder is often played in school today because it is small and easy to carry.

You can learn to play the recorder with a teacher. There are also books to help you learn to play the recorder on your own. This book tells the **musician** which notes to play.

Making a noise

The recorder has three parts. The head has a **mouthpiece** you blow into. The middle has six finger-holes and a thumb-hole. The foot has a hole for the little finger.

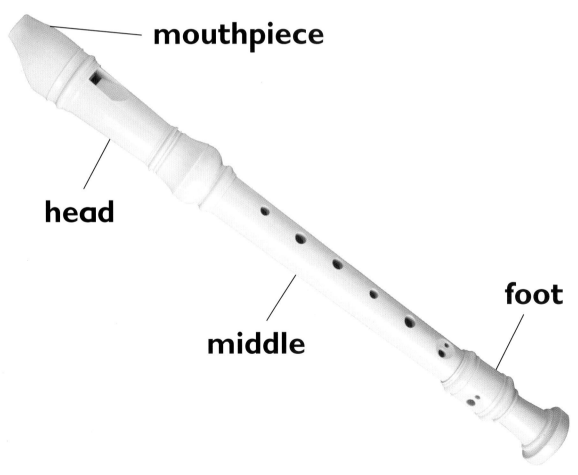

mouthpiece

head

middle

foot

To play the recorder, you blow into the mouthpiece. At the same time, you place your fingers on the finger-holes. This changes the sound. A sound can be high or low. This is called **pitch**.

How the sound is made

When you blow into the recorder, you make the air inside the tube move. This movement is called **vibration**. When air vibrates, it makes a sound.

If you place your fingers on the finger-holes, you trap more air in the tube. This makes the sound lower because the air vibrates more slowly. If you uncover the holes, the sound is higher.

finger-holes

Types of recorder

There are five instruments in the recorder family. The bigger ones have lower **pitch** and the smaller ones higher pitch. The descant recorder is the most popular recorder in school.

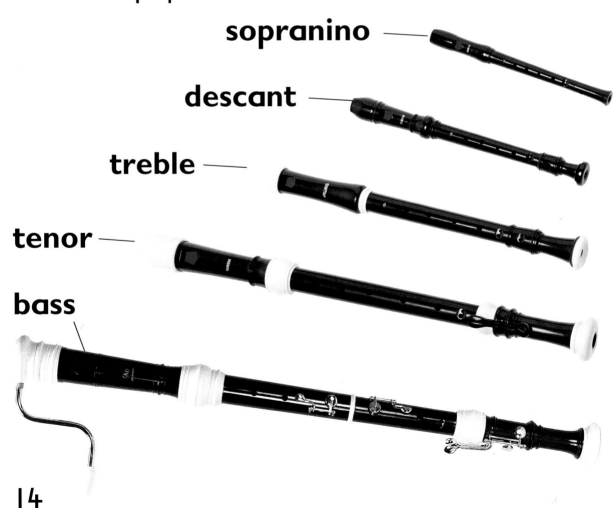

sopranino

descant

treble

tenor

bass

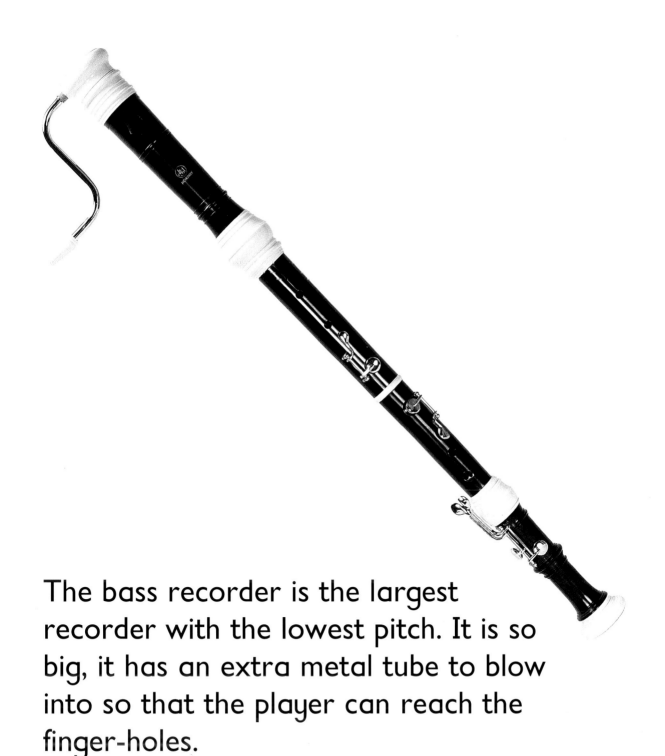

The bass recorder is the largest recorder with the lowest pitch. It is so big, it has an extra metal tube to blow into so that the player can reach the finger-holes.

Recorder concert

You can play the recorder alone. This is called playing **solo**. You can make bird sounds, play sound games or make up your own music with the recorder. You can play songs too.

You can play the recorder in a recorder concert in school or with other woodwind instruments. **Musicians** play the recorder in concerts of old music called **Baroque** music.

Types of woodwind

You play the flute in a different way to the recorder. You blow across the blow hole in the **mouthpiece**. You change **pitch** by pressing down the keys.

Other woodwind instruments have a **reed** in the mouthpiece. A reed is made from a thin strip of cane. When you blow on the reed it **vibrates** making a sound.

Woodwind family

There are other woodwind instruments which make their sound in the same way. The tin whistle **vibrates** inside when we blow into it.

Bagpipes are also woodwind instruments. To play the bagpipes, the player blows air into the bag. The player then squeezes the bag. This forces the air into the pipes. This is what makes the sound.

Around the world

You can find woodwind instruments all over the world. The zurna comes from Turkey. It is like an oboe. Sometimes people play the zurna at weddings.

The pungi comes from India and it is made from a **gourd**. The player blows into one end of the gourd. The sound comes out of two pipes at the other end of the gourd.

Famous music and musicians

You can hear woodwind instruments in a concert **orchestra**. In the music *Peter and the Wolf*, the oboe is used for the Duck and the clarinet for the Cat.

The clarinet and saxophone are also used in **jazz**. Courtney Pine is a famous jazz **musician** who plays the saxophone.

New music

Today, you can hear woodwind instruments in **rock bands**, **pop bands**, **soul** and **heavy metal** music. The tin whistle is often played in Irish pop music.

A **synthesizer** is a keyboard which can **imitate** many different sounds. You can make the sounds of all the woodwind instruments on a synthesizer.

Sound activity

Pour some water into an empty bottle. Blow over the top. You are making the air in the bottle **vibrate**. Pour in some more water and blow again.

Pick a blade of grass and hold it between your thumbs. Blow between your thumbs. The grass vibrates like a **reed** and you can hear a sound.

Thinking about woodwind

You can find the answers to all of these questions in this book.

1. Why are the instruments in this book called woodwind instruments?

2. Which recorder will you most often find in school?

3. Which woodwind instruments can you hear in **jazz** music?

4. What is a pungi?

Glossary

Baroque music written between the years 1600 and 1750
You say *ba-rock*

gourd large fruit with a hard rind
You say *goo-erd*

heavy metal style of loud, energetic, rock music with a strong beat

imitate copy

jazz old style of music from America that is often made up as it is played

mouthpiece part of the instrument placed in or near the mouth

musician someone who plays a musical instrument or sings
You say *mew-zi-shun*

orchestra large group of musicians who play their musical instruments together
You say *or-kes-tra*

pitch the highness or lowness of a sound or musical note

pop bands group of musicians who play music of the last fifty years. A lot of people like this music.

reed thin strip of cane or metal

rock bands group of musicians who play a kind of pop music with a strong beat

solo song or piece of music for one person

soul style of music that is full of feeling. Woodwind instruments are often played in soul music.

synthesizer electronic instrument that can make or change many different sounds
You say *sintha-size-a*

vibrate move up and down or from side to side very quickly

Index